Merry ... 1995

Love,
Susan

RHYMES FROM THE ROUGH

WRITTEN BY

MARGARET KENNARD

DEDICATION

*To my mother — who would have loved
this book, not because she was
a golfer (she wasn't), or an
avid reader (she was), but
because I wrote it!*

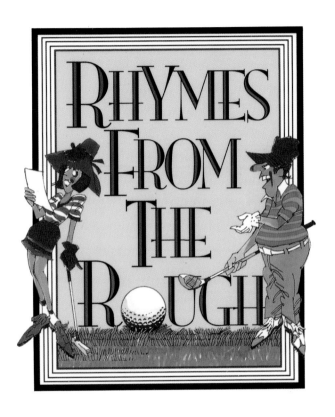

RHYMES FROM THE ROUGH

Published by Golf Gifts, Inc.

Written by
Margaret Kennard

Illustrated by
Chuck Bracke

Published in the United States by
Golf Gifts Publishing Co.
219 Eisenhower Lane South • Lombard, IL 60148

Printed in Hong Kong

ISBN: 1-878728-23-7

1 2 3 4 5 6 7 8 9 10

Printing/AK/Year 98 97 96 95 94 93 92

INTRODUCTION

This book is dedicated to all the duffers and weekend players who thoroughly love the game of golf, and who, despite set-backs, keep going back for more. Having once thought chasing a small white object with an awkward steel stick a silly occupation, I now have the rabid enthusiasm of the convert.

Unlike tennis, where the player bakes on clay or all weather synthetic, I walk (or, if lucky, ride) on springy green turf under the shade of the spreading chestnut, oak, maple or whatever miserable tree the Machiavellian course designer has come up with.

Glorious vistas stretch out before me, filling my soul with the joy of being alive (and my mind with fear of that rather wide-looking lake). What does it matter if there's a sand trap or two? Hope springs eternal, and I know that this time my drives will be straight and long, my chips accurate, and putts true.

And isn't that what keeps us all going back?

TABLE OF CONTENTS

Chapter One..............................8
Looking It Over

Chapter Two............................ 13
Free Admission

Chapter Three.........................22
The Breaks Of The Game

Chapter Four...........................28
The Romance Of Golf

Chapter Five............................36
Fore-Cast

Chapter Six..............................43
Sigh-Cology

Chapter Seven........................50
Nursery Versery

Chapter Eight..........................59
Adding It Up

GOLF

The Scottish invented it,
Wives have resented it,
T.V.'s presented it,
Weather's prevented it,
Duffers have often learned
*   to repent of it,*
Pros, on the other hand, seem
*   quite content with it,*
What other game could bring
*   so much dissent to it*
Making you curse the money
*   you spent on it...*
What other game
*   except golf?*

CHAPTER ONE

LOOKING IT OVER

On Looking Down The Fairway
or
Color Me Yellow

Just like a picture postcard,
So green it's almost fake...
But I could do without
*   the blue*
That tells me there's a lake!

TREES

With Kilmer's praises
I agree...
Except when standing
on the tee!

Sandbagged

Whether you call it
A bunker or trap,
If your ball lands there
You must take the rap...
You can grit your teeth,
But don't ground your club,
You can swear or pray,
But just don't flub...
For there's always some wag
Who will slyly preach,
"You're too old to be playing
On the beach!"

CHAPTER TWO

FREE ADMISSION

Golf Bunt

I never hook,
I seldom slice,
My ball goes straight
    and true...
My only fault
Is that the yards
I drive it are so few!

HELP!
or
Why the Nineteenth Hole Does Good Business

I stand on the tee determinedly
With all of my lessons in mind;
My feet are in place with just the
*   right space,*
My hands on the club intertwined...
I line up with care so the clubhead
*   is square,*
My eye's on the ball as I pivot;
But what can I do, when despite
*   follow-through,*
What travels the most is my divot?!

Wood(s) Shot

The sound of wood against
the ball
Is very satisfying,
Until the sound of ball
on wood
Sends all my par hopes
flying!

Handicap

It isn't ten or twenty,
It isn't scratch or three...
My handicap in golf,
I fear,
Happens to be me!

Not Up To Scratch

My clubs are the finest
That money can buy,
The price of my outfit
Would make bankers cry,
The golf balls I carry
Are meant to go far,
But I can't beg or borrow
A score close to par!

On The Green

It isn't that I always choose
The gentlemanly role,
Unfortunately,
*   I'm the one*
Who's farthest from
*   the hole!*

LONG SHOT

To drive the ball three
    hundred yards
Is what I do just fine,
My chief chagrin is it's
    not in
The fairway that is mine!

CHAPTER THREE

THE BREAKS OF THE GAME

TEED OFF!

There's nothing makes me
    quite so cross
As letting foursomes
    through,
Who then proceed to lose
    a ball
And hunt it while I stew!

Putt Guts

He claims that it's a gimme
Every time we play,
Whether it's an inch or two
Or several feet away!

Unwanted Audience

It makes me upset and
*   embarrassed*
When the foursome behind
*   me arrive*
Just in time for my stellar
*   performance*
As I wallop a fifty-foot drive!

Contrast

The faces on the starting tee
Show keen anticipation,
There are lots of jokes and
          practice strokes —
A scene of relaxation...
At green eighteen,
          those faces seem
Much sadder than before —
It isn't age — they're just
          more sage
Because they know
          the score!

CHAPTER FOUR

THE ROMANCE OF GOLF

Cocktail Party Hero

If, right after his name,
He begins on his game —
Citing scores that make
     other men cry,
I'm afraid the effect
Is to make me suspect
What is known as a
     terrible lie!

LESSON

The honeymoon is over,
She thinks that he's a louse,
She should have known
*   you never take*
Golf lessons from
*   your spouse!*

Un-Fair Game

I'm off to a party —
I can't wait to go,
I have a new dress that I'm
    longing to show;
I've planned and I've planned
From my shoes to my hair,
I think I'll be dashing,
And make the men stare...
I'm now at the party —
And where are the men?
In the kitchen dissecting
Their golf games again!

Pre-Nuptial Agreement

Before you contemplate
    "I do,"
Before you set the date,
There's one small question
    you should ask
Of your intended mate...
For it will save a lot of fuss
When weekend time comes
    due,
If you've agreed where he
    will be —
Out golfing or with you?

WHIFFED OPPORTUNITY

I met him at a party —
It was romance at first sight,
We had many things
*   in common —*
Golf was one, to my delight...
So we made a golf
*   engagement*
That I sadly must repine,
For he never followed through
When I scored seventy
*   for nine!*

Golf Widow

I sit at home
Eating lunch alone
Not because I'm unfriendly
    or plain,
But because my mate
Has his weekly date
For golf, come sunshine
    or rain!

CHAPTER FIVE

FORE-CAST

Water Hazard

The weekly golf league
meets today,
And if I needed proof,
I only have to listen to
The rain upon my roof!

Weekend Plans

It's Saturday morning,
A lovely Spring day —
Just perfect for painting
Or clearing away...
The lark's in the treetop,
The squirrel's in the
    shrubs,
And Dad's in the wagon
Loading his clubs!

WORK WEAK

The calendar says Friday,
The clock says
    half past two,
But in the business offices
There's no male left in view;
Where are these business
    magnates
Who control our destiny?
They're lining up their
    golf carts
On the very first tee!

Inclement Weather

It's much too hot
to mow the lawn
Or weed the flower bed,
The only thing it's fit for
Is a round of golf instead!

Second-Hand Vacation

There's snow on the ground
And frost on the pane —
A typical mid-winter day,
But the tube takes me where
It's sunny and fair,
Watching the golf
    pros at play!

CHAPTER SIX

SIGH-COLOGY

Perfect Lie

Playing golf is easy
As anyone can see,
Especially when you're lying
In an armchair by T.V.

Solo Performance

When I'm playing
    with friends
For a wager or two,
Why can't I putt it
As well as I do
On the rug in the office
With no one in view!

The Mystery Of Golf

If golf is so relaxing,
If golf is so much fun,
Why are so many tempers
*   worse*
When once the game is
*   done?*

Out Of
My League

Beware the invitational
To someone else's course,
For though it sounds sensational
I've learned to my remorse,
That faced with a terrain
That I have never seen before,
And a group whose games
*   (to hear them talk)*
Should have them all on tour,
The confidence I've nurtured
Simply vanishes and dies,
As I build a monumental score
That earns the booby prize!

Bogus Bravado

Just when you think you've
mastered it,
Just when you think
you're fine,
Just when you think
there's nothing
To that par three
number nine...
Just when you're
feeling confident
A birdie will be yours,
Up leaps that bogey-man
called nerves
Producing bogey scores!

CHAPTER SEVEN

NURSERY VERSERY

No Laughing Matter

Old King Cole
Was a merry old soul,
And a merry old
*   soul was he...*
Till he got quite miffed
On the day he whiffed
And left his ball on the tee!

Lost Ball

Oh where, oh where has
my little ball gone,
Oh where, oh where
can it be?
I hit it quite nice
Till it curved in a slice,
And I'm now hitting
three from the tee!

SPECTATOR SPORT

Little Miss Muffet
Sat on a tuffet
Watching the Pro-Am
play...
Till, instead of a spider,
A ball fell beside her
And frightened Miss
Muffet away!

Wet Blanket

Rain, rain, go away;
Come again another day,
My golf foursome
* wants to play!*

PUTT OUT

Mary had a little putt —
She needed it
   for par;
Mary has a second putt —
The first one went
   too far!

Landscape Artistry

*Here we go round the
    mulberry bush
Someone planted with
    loving care,
While we hope in vain
Someone else will claim
The ball that is nestled
    there!*

Headache

Jack and Jill
Went up the hill
To play the long par five;
Jack came down
With a broken crown
For laughing at Jill's
*   short drive!*

ADDING IT UP

CERTIFIED PRIVATE ACCOUNTANTS

Over the river and
*   through the wood*
To the eighteenth
*   green we go,*
And if some detours
Are not on our scores
Only our caddies
*   will know!*

Objectively
Speaking
or
A Non-Player Looks
at Golf

Isn't it ridiculous —
How crazy can you be
To try to hit a small white sphere
From something called a tee
Across a vast expanse of land
Three hundred yards or more —
With lovely woods and scenic streams
You hopefully ignore —
Just to reach a tiny hole
Not quite five inches wide,
And with a sigh of great relief
To make that small ball slide
Into the cup so that you can
Begin the whole thing once again!

ABOUT THE AUTHOR

Margaret Kennard, who likes to be called "Maggie," is a native of Baltimore, Maryland who migrated to Cincinnati, Ohio after college. Married to an Englishman whom she met in Bermuda, Maggie has spent most of her career close to the written word—working in advertising, greeting card editing, and now as a free-lance writer. She loves working with words and has written everything from directions on how to home permanent your hair to architect manuals to lyrics for sales videos. "If it needs words, I'll take it on!"

But her love is humorous verse. In this book, she draws on her experience in two ladies' golf leagues, which shall remain nameless to protect the innocent! "I couldn't find a tennis partner and was coerced into golf, with which I had a love/hate relationship!" Both show up here, as she pokes gentle fun at the frustrations most of us have experienced on the golf course.